A Thoughtful Gospel

Living Out God's Story Today

Mark Moore
&
David Timms

Oak Tree Press
Rocklin, CA

Library of Congress Cataloging-in-Publication Data
Mark Moore & David Timms
A Thoughtful Gospel: Living Out God's Story Today

ISBN-13: 979-8-397-53923-4

1. *Bible* 2. *Theology* 3. *Church Resources* 4. *Apologetics* 5. *Worldview*

Printed in the United States of America

Cover Design: Stephanie VanTassell (stephvt@me.com)

Oak Tree Press
The mighty oak tree, barren in the winter but vibrant in the Spring, stands as a glorious metaphor for human life in the hands of God.

Table of Contents

Introduction

It's obvious. The Christian community in Western culture has grown increasingly secularized and decreasingly literate about Scripture and faith. Both surveys and conversations affirm this reality. We have either ceased to think or spent too much time thinking wrongly, and the prognosis is not good.

Back in the 1960s, the cynical and aging British philosopher Bertrand Russell mockingly declared, "Most Christians would rather die than think—in fact they do." Three decades later, in 1994, Os Guinness wrote his penetrating book *Fit Bodies, Fat Minds: Why Evangelicals Don't Think and What to Do About It.* He analyzed not just the anti-intellectualism of so many Christians but the cultural developments that were rendering them ethically and morally comatose when it came to faith and its relevance to culture and life.

Many subsequent authors and speakers have reinforced this same theme because the continued decline is all too evident. Evangelicalism, once a movement with strong biblical teaching and deep theological convictions has, in some places, devolved into a right-wing political voting bloc that has either forgotten or abandoned biblical values in favor of cultural pragmatism. The priorities seem to be, "Who will get the stock market soaring again so that our retirement accounts are strong? And who will take us back to the simpler days of Mayberry and *The Andy Griffith Show* when issues of sexual identity, racism, police funding, terrorism, mass shootings, critical race theory, and biomedical ethics were just *not* issues?"

Many older evangelicals pine for simpler days — the dubiously good old days — because they don't want to (or don't have the tools to) think deeply and Christianly about the world in which we live. Meanwhile, many others who profess to be Christians have been deceived into embracing *moralistic therapeutic deism* without even realizing it. Sociologists Christian Smith and Melinda Lundquist Denton first coined this phrase in 2005 following interviews with over 3,000 young adults about their religious beliefs. In short, it holds to four tenets:

1. God wants us to be nice to each other.
2. Life is about happiness and feeling good about ourselves.
3. If we do the right thing, God will show up and fix our problems when we need him to.
4. Good people go to heaven when they die.

This pervasive spiritual worldview is a strange mixture of Hinduism ("What goes around comes around" also known as *karma*), Deism ("There is a God but he's not here, near, or engaged"), and Christianity ("Eternity is real and heaven exists").

The dangerous simplism of this kind of false gospel cannot be overstated. It is extraordinarily narcissistic, and relegates God to the role of our occasional therapist or (worse) water boy. In this spiritual distortion, God sits quietly in the wings waiting for us to summon him for help; not terribly interested in anything deeper, richer, or better than that. Furthermore, the highest purpose of this false gospel is discovering God's personal plan and blessing for my own life. It's all about *me*. I'm the central figure of the story, and God is the supporting actor at best.

Thus, on the one hand, God is disengaged from our everyday experiences, and functions as our occasional crisis counselor or divine first responder. On the other hand, as long as we are decent human beings, it's God's job to steer us towards success and prosperity. It's little wonder that the "Christian mind" has become a rare sighting in our day. We let others think for us, and we allow powerful or wealthy people (stars and celebrities) to become our primary arbiters of ethics (telling us what is good and right).

Needless to say, this is no small matter, and the consequences impact us both now and possibly for eternity.

Many cultural analysts have noted the decline of the church and the seemingly inexorable decline of Christian influence in western culture. Surveys and polls repeatedly reveal dramatic drops in biblical literacy. People just don't read or know their Bibles as folk once did. In some places Christian faith has become so politicized that political figures have greater influence than pastors, and political convictions override biblical or spiritual beliefs.

There's plenty to wring our hands about, but perhaps the greatest danger to Christian influence is our growing inability to think Christianly. In other words, we may listen to sermons, broadcasts, and podcasts for years without developing a worldview that helps us assess issues and concerns for ourselves. We start to parrot our favorite primetime cable presenters or radio personalities, and find ourselves washed along in the froth and foam of our culture without a way to think differently or to think for ourselves.

That's why we are writing this short book. We believe there is a simple but powerful way to reframe conversations. We believe that the story of the Bible, which is much more memorable than a page of Bible verses, provides God's wisdom and gives us insight into every significant topic of our day.

Historically, Christians have tended to try and find a Bible verse here and there that says something closely related to their concern. If you are wondering what the Bible says about giving, type "giving" into some Bible software and see if it gives you some verses that might be helpful, even if there is no consideration for the original context. This approach to thinking Christianly has obvious limitations. If we find a verse that says "The poor will always be with you" (Matthew 26:11), it might be enough to make us apathetic about poverty and its commensurate suffering. Random verses are a poor way to build a systematic worldview.

This book is for you if you want to think more deeply, more consistently, more biblically, and therefore more Christianly.

When Jesus came and called people to *repent*, he was urging them to literally "change their mind." When we follow Christ, we resolve to think differently and subsequently act differently. And as we lean more into him, the Holy Spirit renews our minds (Romans 12:2).

Please note that the chapters of this book are only a primer; an introduction. We won't go into a deep academic analysis of various worldviews. James Sire (*The Universe Next Door*) and others have done a great job of that already. We want to simply propose a model—and story—that could help you have deeper and richer conversations with friends and family than you might have imagined possible. Our hope is that this book is a conversation starter, not the whole conversation.

In short, the opening few chapters will set the table for the story; the thoughtful gospel. We'll briefly establish both the existence of and the need for objective truth. Biblical truth provides a consistent anchor for our worldview formation. We'll frame this conversation around thinking critically while also listening compassionately. Our culture seems to have lost the capacity for both of these. Then we'll walk through the six episodes or acts of the biblical story and show how they speak to virtually every issue and concern that we have today. Finally, we'll apply this gospel worldview to some specific issues to illustrate how this simple framework can help us make flourishing life choices with consistency and clarity, even when we face complex contemporary issues and ideologies.

Chapter One

What is Truth?

On January 3, 2023 a freshly elected United States Congress convened. It included a new Republican member for New York's third congressional district, Representative George Santos. Within weeks, news outlets were aflame with stories about him. The 34-year-old had a story and a resume that did not add up; one which nobody had bothered to check deeply before the previous November election.

Santos, aka Anthony Devolder, spoke of being Jewish. He wasn't. He claimed his mother died as a result of 9/11. Immigration records suggest she wasn't even in the country at that time. He said that his maternal grandparents escaped the holocaust. They didn't. He spoke of graduating from Baruch College. He never attended there. He boasted of leading Baruch's men's volleyball team to a championship, and requiring double knee surgery thereafter. He didn't. He claimed to have worked for Citigroup and Goldman Sachs. He never did. Old acquaintances of Santos said he had competed as a drag queen in Brazil as a 20-year-old. He denied it; then changed his story.

He claimed to have funded his own election campaign with $500,000 of his own money, but changed his story when asked how he ever made that much money. He denied any criminal charges against him (for check theft and forgery) in Brazil, until Brazilian authorities reinstated charges once they "found their man" because he was in the news.

These and a staggering number of other lies piled higher than almost anything anyone had seen in living memory. Meanwhile, Santos steadfastly refused to resign from Congress despite countless protests and calls for him to do so. But more shockingly, the Republican Speaker of the House proceeded to reward the new Congressional representative with two committee positions.

Santos called many of his blatant lies mere *embellishments*. "Who hasn't padded their resume?" he asked. However, the sheer weight of his deceit, dishonesty, and lack of integrity left even former friends dumbfounded. In the face of all of this Santos barely blushed and insisted that his new political power was independent of any personal history. He suggested that character and truth were inconsequential to him performing his duties as a public servant. And apparently many of his congressional colleagues felt the same way.

This story illustrates perfectly how confused and compromised we have become about truth. As a culture, we have traded truth for expediency and relegated truth to a quaint value of the past. It has taken a beating and is barely or rarely driving our choices.

We do not stand on truth. Instead, we have often reduced truth to mean nothing more than a personal conviction or perspective: "It's true if it's true *to you*." Sometimes truth has been obscured by spin or obfuscation. Other times we have assumed that truth is measured by how loud, proud, or brash a person might be. We have forgotten that truth is not measured by decibels but by accuracy. The moon is not made of cheese, no matter how long or hard I might insist on it; no matter what I might read or retweet.

This is not the place to enter into a deep philosophical analysis of truth, though we might reasonably assert that a true theory or belief must be congruent with our experience, internally consistent (and not fail the Law of Non-Contradiction), coherent with everything else that we know, and be useful for organizing our thinking and practice. While this might be a generally useful set of principles for the philosopher and the scientist, truth also has pragmatic and relational significance. Pragmatism: Does this work? Relationships: Can

I trust this person? That is, truth allows us to function meaningfully in the world and with other people. If we lose our grip on truth we lose our grip on everything, and therein lies the clue to a major conundrum of our day.

We have grown disturbingly comfortable with lies and dishonesty; violations of truth. People no longer lie (we're told); they simply exaggerate or embellish. Or, if they do lie, they are excused because of their heritage, circumstances, age, power, or personality. It's apparently okay, understandable, and excusable to lie if we feel threatened or uncomfortable.

In one poll of "least trusted" (least truthful) professions in the United States, people rated the following six professions as least trusted.

1. Members of Congress
2. Car Salespeople
3. Advertising Practitioners
4. Business Executives
5. Lawyers
6. Journalists

We have reached a very low point in the history of western civilization. And yet, while we harbor deep doubts and skepticism about certain professions, dishonesty has become normalized for all of us. Perhaps it's because we all want the freedom to be dishonest without judgment. Yet, such freedom is no freedom at all. Our culture wants tolerance without responsibility, and niceness without accountability. Truth might be a casualty, but we are the ultimate victims.

Two thousand years ago, in an extraordinarily tense drama, Jesus told the Roman Governor Pilate that he had come to "bear witness to the truth," to which Pilate asked, "What is truth?" (John 18:37-38) People have grappled with that question throughout the ages.

When we talk about truth there are several key elements to consider.

First, truth frequently involves facts. Facts certainly form part of the truth, but truth is much larger than facts. For example, we might truthfully say that H_2O is the common molecular formula for water and that the continental United States is bordered by Mexico and Canada. These are facts, and they are relatively easy to establish and prove. At the most superficial level, truth often depends on facts.

Second, truth is about greater realities than mere facts. For example, what can we say about the existence and character of God? We might want to declare categorically that God exists and that he is loving and gracious, but these are *derived* truths based on observation and interpretation of peripheral or secondary matters. We might appeal to the testimony, observations, and experiences of other people throughout history or even our own experiences, but these are not empirical facts. We can count the number of tickets sold for a ball game, but the grace of God is not something we can measure, test, or repeat using the scientific method. It doesn't make it less true, but it is a truth of a different kind.

It is this second category of truth that usually generates the greatest skepticism or conflict, because inherent in *these* truth claims is a particular amount of interpretation. My certainty might be your skepticism. It's easy to see why this category of truth has become a casualty of our individualism and decreasing convictions.

At some point, we must either accept that common ethics are an unrealistic ideal or we must identify a benchmark — a standard — which will govern our collective life.

Over the last twenty centuries, western cultures in particular have typically embraced a Judeo-Christian worldview. By that, cultural and spiritual leaders mean that the Bible and the Church have provided the foundational benchmarks for ethical decision-making. They have shaped the legal system, motivated the rise of healthcare, undergirded education, and influenced communities wherever they formed. The Judeo-Christian worldview led ultimately to the abolition of slavery and child labor practices, and the development of countless non-profit agencies and organizations serving around the world.

Granted, Christians have divided with painful regularity over interpretations of the Bible, particularly since the Renaissance and the Reformation. Nevertheless, until recent generations, western civilization has embraced a basic foundation, a bedrock on which to build. The Bible provided this framework for viewing the world. As such it helped address the questions about origins, meaning, morality, and destiny. That's what worldviews do. A worldview always provides an answer to these deeper existential questions about where we come from, why we are here, why we matter, how we should live, and what happens after death. And once we establish these existential truths, they influence our actions, values, and morals in significant ways.

For example, if we conclude that there is no God, that humanity is just a random evolutionary adaptation of the animal kingdom, that we are as subject to "survival of the fittest" as any other species, and that there is nothing beyond the grave, it makes each of us the center of our own world. We have no ethical basis to appeal for sympathy or compassion, or to expect equality or fairness. We have no objective basis for objection to corruption, sexual abuse, dishonesty, or violence. We might not want or like those things done to us, but we cannot legitimately expect others to be restrained. In this worldview, nobody can be governed by the standards or expectations of others. It's a free-for-all.

We might consider "our truth" to be reasonable and even beneficial, but without a common standard, we can only hope others might agree with us. The outcome is obvious; the very anarchy and chaos that looms large on our cultural horizon right now. In the absence of a standard for truth, everyone does what is right in their own eyes, and "what is right" generally means whatever benefits us most in the moment as individuals.

Laws and law enforcement are only so helpful. If we reject the basis for law, then we are likely to live lawlessly with each other. For example, speed limit signs have become suggestions not limitations in the minds of many drivers today. If we shared a worldview that extolled social responsibility, mutual accountability, and conscientious obedience, drivers might be more attentive to posted signs. But where the prevailing worldview promotes personal autonomy, social independence, and individualism, we're much more likely to see drivers traveling whatever speed they prefer.

Truth is neither random nor concocted. There is truth, and it comes from a stable and reliable source. That source is God himself. He sends his Son ("the Word" according to John 1:1) who perfectly embodies and models truth in human life, and gives us his written word (Scripture) as a record of truth.

If we do not agree that there is absolute and objective truth that comes from a source beyond ourselves, then the rest of this book will make little sense. But Jesus truthfully declared "I am the Way, the Truth, and the Life" (John 14:6), so the path to the flourishing life clearly winds to him, through him, and from him. We believe that what he said is true.

Chapter Two

Thinking Critically and Listening Compassionately

Despite the counter-claims and protests, not all worldviews have equal validity or value.

Secularism, which specifically excludes God from all discussion and consideration, struggles to provide meaningful common ground for moral and ethical living. **Humanism**, which makes human life and experience the central and dominant consideration for determining the good, the true, and the beautiful, cannot account for the profound limitations of our brokenness, isolation, and corruption. **Capitalism**, an economic model and worldview, insists on individual freedoms and rights that can easily slide towards greed and selfish competition. **Socialism**, which insists on communities sharing resources equally (enforced distributive justice), can demotivate a work ethic and foster corruption among those who must manage the resources.

We could march through a long list of contemporary worldviews and ideologies and easily identify significant flaws and limitations in each one.

On the one hand, we might feel overwhelmed by the options and conclude that everyone must just decide for themselves how they will view and interpret the world, and live their lives. This happens all the time. It can feel like *worldview overload*, and we might check our brains at the door because we feel that we have no capacity to assess or evaluate the ideologies that swirl around us.

On the other hand, we might grow contemptuous of other people because of the way that they choose to approach life and live their lives. Such contempt has a way of isolating us and shutting down any meaningful conversation. The family just rolls its eyes about "crazy old Uncle George!" It is easy in a culture that breeds and affirms contempt—just listen to groups on the political right and left fringes—to scoff at the apparent ignorance of people whose worldview differs from our own. Yet, perhaps we forget that worldview is formed from complex factors.

Our worldview is the product of *at least* the following sources:

1. Our family background, experiences, and implicit values;

2. Broader cultural practices and pressures that surround us;
3. The powerful values that emanate from our preferred media sources;
4. Our teachers and education;
5. The friendship groups we establish and their significant peer influence;
6. Key authors, bloggers, or podcasters in our lives;
7. Entertainment that we choose to watch and absorb (music, film, video games, etc.).

These factors are deeply formative and often shape us in ways we neither realize nor easily identify. For the most part it happens unconsciously. For example, we don't know that we are gradually normalizing and embracing violence as we watch certain media or play certain games, but it is happening. We think we are just being entertained, but we are actually being formed. That's the subtlety we experience *every day*.

Consequently, it takes an enormous amount of discipline, intentionality, consistency, and courage to swim upstream; to go against the tide. Nobody finds that easy.

For believers, the Bible (God's revealed truth) has a foundational impact on our worldview as the

Holy Spirit illuminates God's truth to us. Christians have the God-given, grace-shaped opportunity for renewed minds, unlike the minds of unbelievers which are blinded by the god of this world (2 Corinthians 4:4).

That leads us to the title of this chapter. As we get serious about identifying, understanding, and embracing a gospel worldview, we will also want to be specific and intentional about thinking critically and listening compassionately to people whose worldviews differ from our own. These two qualities must complement each other as we grow. Here's why.

Thinking Critically

The gospel worldview is not just one option among many equal options from which to choose. If worldviews are not all equally valid or valuable, then we need to have a clear basis for assessing why we would choose or discard a particular orientation to life. This is what we mean by *thinking critically*. We consider deeply, analyze thoughtfully, and choose wisely.

The *gospel worldview* provides a powerful benchmark for our analysis and assessment of secularism, humanism, socialism, hedonism, capitalism, and all of the other *-isms* of our day. The truths inherent and core to the gospel worldview, as we unpack it and understand more of it, will make syncretism of worldviews less and less possible or plausible. We'll discover that the Way of Jesus and the teaching of the Bible is actually antithetical to some of the core tenets of other worldviews—even the other religious worldviews—of our day.

Jesus famously declared of himself: "I am the way, the truth, and the life. No one comes to the Father but through me" (John 14:6). This statement of exclusivity has distinguished the Christian faith from all other major world religions. Jesus was clearly *not* presenting the gospel or himself as a potential addendum to other religious ideas. He was explicitly coming to replace them. Any "Jesus plus" philosophy or worldview is not Jesus at all. Similarly, the gospel worldview does not make room for syncretism. God does not invite us to mix-and-match great teachings of the past with the loudest voices of our day, to decide how to live. The Creator has a design and plan for human flourishing and he has revealed that plan to us. We cannot create a competing blueprint for flourishing and expect it to work. That would produce a knock-off life at best; no quality or authenticity about it.

Of course, in a world that takes offense at claims of exclusivity, this is anathema. And yet it makes total sense. Can you imagine the car maker BMW simply saying to customers that they'll provide an array of car and tractor parts for their clients to buy what they like and assemble how they like so that they can drive one of the world's safest and best motor vehicles? Of course not. BMW have blueprints for their vehicles right down to the most minor details, and often require highly trained technicians if the final result is to be a sports vehicle rather than a bizarre tractor-car of our own design and making. Why would it not be the same with God, our Creator. If we reject the exclusive and intricate blueprint plans of the Creator because exclusivity sounds arrogant, we are implicitly rejecting the final product that the Designer always intended. Simple as that. Exclusivity is not about arrogance but about the glorious and rich fulfillment of God's perfect design and purpose for humanity.

With this in mind, the gospel worldview (which tells God's story, plan, and purpose for each of us) thus becomes the benchmark for critically evaluating the alternative worldviews of our day. For example, if the gospel worldview is grounded in the sanctity of life, then philosophies and values that would demean this sanctity of life might reasonably be resisted and rejected.

It is not only irrational to believe that all worldviews have equal validity and value, it is disorienting and dangerous. Human beings cannot simultaneously be both sacred (made in the image of God) and no higher than slugs in the garden. There are enormous consequences and implications each way.

That's why this little book is significant, from our perspective. The more familiar we become with the gospel worldview, the easier we will recognize the counterfeit and destructive values of our culture. If we have a way to identify and describe the pitfalls of other ideologies, we will become more confident of our own worldview. Some views of life are oil and water; utterly incompatible. We cannot be created *for* a purpose and *with* a purpose and simultaneously be the accidental product of evolutionary development. Life cannot be both sacred and meaningless. Truth cannot be both absolute and relative. Eternity cannot be both something and nothing. Compassion cannot be both essential and optional. Power cannot be for both service and exploitation. And so on.

The gospel worldview will allow us to look beneath the hood of the world's philosophies and understand better what we are looking at.

There is a flip side to all of this. After all, it would be possible to read the preceding pages and imagine that we are stoking the fires of a fresh culture war. Evangelicals in the United States have witnessed this culture war mentality since at least the 1980s, and it generally isolates us and gives rise to echo chambers that undermine authentic conversation. We find ourselves only "preaching to the choir." Thus, we want to insist that the gospel worldview encourages us to also *listen compassionately.*

Listening Compassionately

Our family, friends, and neighbors are not our enemies. They may hold to different convictions and values, but they are generally the unconscious product of their own environment or spiritually blinded by "the god of this world" (2 Corinthians 4:3-4), as we are, until we become more specifically intentional about the way of Jesus. Thus, the path forward is to learn to listen compassionately.

Some people will argue against this. "Compassion," they suggest "might be misconstrued as tacit agreement." Others fear that genuinely listening to other people — seeking first to understand before being understood — might minimize our sense of urgency or importance.

Apologetics has frequently functioned this way, to its detriment. Christian apologists have sometimes tried to batter down intellectual doors that might have been gently opened had they taken a more gracious approach and knocked gently rather than charged in with a battering ram.

Jesus came into a first-century culture that was every bit as polluted, corrupted, and confused as our own. Poverty, violence, and immorality could be found everywhere; especially wherever the Romans left their occupying stamp. Indeed, part of what made Jesus' famous Sermon on the Mount (Matthew 5-7) so startling and significant is that it defied so many of the core values and teachings of the day. Yet, Jesus did not roll into town and set out to debate and defeat all comers. Yes, he entered some conflicted conversation with various Pharisees and other Jewish religious leaders, but Jesus' dominant posture with people was grace, gentleness, attentiveness, and wisdom. He did not mold his message to accommodate false thinking, but he generally listened compassionately before he clarified the truth for his listeners. We would do well to embrace this same posture.

We want to invite you to embrace an attitude of hospitality as you read through this book and consider your friends and family. Hospitality does not mean agreement with them or indifference about them. Rather, it means adopting a heart to listen compassionately not condescendingly. What's right about our neighbor's thinking? And what is clearly wrong? What might be helpful about our colleague's perspective? And what might be damaging? Let's choose not to jump to conclusions about *their* views, but to listen well, ask thoughtful and gentle questions, and understand deeply. Very few people have changed their minds by being beaten into submission. Most of us gradually see the light through love, compassion, and gentleness.

For us, this is an important posture. If this book breeds apologetic warriors, we will have failed. We hope instead that you will enter a journey of gracious companionship with those whom the Lord leads to you. Yes, the conviction that Christ guides us daily is part of the gospel worldview. Let's start to unpack that worldview now.

Chapter Three

A Gospel Worldview

We come now to the heart of this book. How might we think more Christianly?

Given that there is a set of absolute truths that should govern the flourishing life, and assuming that we want to move beyond thoughtless tolerance that simply reinforces aberrant thinking and perpetuates human suffering, is there a system or structure that could help us move towards healing and authentic hope? We think so.

Over time many people have talked about embracing a Christian worldview. Some people have used the phrase biblical worldview. We are proposing a different option: gospel worldview. Here's why.

When we talk about *Christian worldview*, it begs the question: Which Christian worldview? That might sound like an odd question, but there are, in fact, a multitude of Christian beliefs that exist and that differ from group to group. By Christian, would we mean Roman Catholic with its special emphasis on family responsibility, papal authority, traditionalism, or even (in some parts of the world) syncretism with local religions? Or might we mean Orthodoxy, which has its own set of sub-beliefs about community, marriage, the saints, etc.? Or perhaps someone means evangelical Christianity, or Pentecostal Christianity, or Reformed Christianity, or yet some other branch with its own doctrinal particularities. The worldview of the Christian Amish community is vastly different from the worldview of gun-toting evangelical believers in the American south. The assumption that there is uniformity of belief and worldview under the simple rubric of Christian would be perhaps misguided.

Similarly, the phrase *biblical worldview* presents some challenges if we dig ever so slightly below the surface. Which biblical worldview do we mean? Religious Jews today might claim a biblical worldview based on their adherence to what we call the Old Testament. Within the biblical record, there is a vast array of possibilities. If we embrace the worldview of Abraham and others, we might endorse polygamy. If we embrace the worldview of the ancient prophets we might develop a "favored nation" theology and perhaps even expect the physical restoration of the nation and land of Israel and the Temple. If we land just on a handful of New Testament texts, we might believe that life is all about discovering and exercising our spiritual gifts and living constantly in the world of signs and wonders. Or others might see life as marked by spiritual warfare at every turn. Still others might become preoccupied with the second coming of Christ (as the believers at Thessalonica did) and decide to quit their jobs and just wait for Jesus to return. These are all arguably biblical worldviews, in the broadest sense that they are reflected (rightly or wrongly) by people in the Bible. The assumption that everyone throughout the Bible embraced and modeled a unified worldview might be difficult to demonstrate. This is not to say that the Bible is full of inconsistencies, but that people have not always consistently understood or modeled the purpose and plan of God from creation.

Consequently, we have chosen to embrace and propose the phrase *gospel worldview* for two reasons.

First, the gospel is not tied to the idiosyncrasies of biblical cultures throughout the ages. Each period and each group of people in the biblical narrative, even with their shortcomings or limitations, point to the messianic age. Thus, the messianic age (the good news and good time for which everyone longed) would help define what was right or not right about the previous Jewish worldview. The gospel therefore becomes the yardstick for measuring all other biblical worldviews. If something does not align with the gospel, then it is an imperfect practice, not an exemplar for us.

Second, we have chosen the phrase gospel worldview precisely because the gospel is not simply a set of propositions or rules to believe but a narrative, a story, into which we enter and live. A story forms a far better basis for evaluating life — even our own lives — than a list of rules or doctrinal declarations. We think that story has always been particularly powerful throughout human history as a primary means to evaluate our own lives and beliefs.

Cultures have always gathered around campfires or dinner tables and told stories. Some of those stories (think of family legends) have been told and repeated not just for entertainment but specifically to reinforce a truth about life. When we are in conversation with each other, trying to evaluate whether something is good or right, we often share our own stories of success or failure to get clarity. Stories speak to us differently than "Ten Truths for a Godly Marriage" or "Six Steps to Career Success." The lists have a place, but stories tend to rise above lists in helpfulness.

As we use the word story, please bear in mind that this is not simply a story in the sense that the ancient slave and storyteller Aesop used to write moral and ethical stories (based on animals) around 600 BC. The gospel story is not conjecture or simply wise insights. It is absolutely true. It is his story — God's story. History is, after all, in its best versions, the telling of God's story and humanity's part in it.

Yes, the gospel is a story. Indeed, the whole story of the Bible forms the gospel story; from creation to the final consummation of all things and the launch of a new heaven and a new earth. Our understanding of the story, and our increasing understanding of its intricacies and nuances, can help us form a worldview that will lead to a flourishing life. That would be good news indeed.

This gospel story — the entire story of the Bible — might be accurately told in just six acts, or six chapters, or six stages. It's a story with six parts that might be most memorable if we use some alliteration. Here it is in short, and we'll unpack each act with a little more detail in the following six chapters.

1. Creation
2. Conflict
3. Covenant

4.   Christ
5.   Church
6.   Consummation

These six "Cs" help make it easier to recall, and if we can lock these in place, we'll be able to tell the entire story of the Bible in just sixty seconds. Here it is in a single paragraph.

> God CREATED the world and us with a plan and purpose but we rebelled against him and entered into CONFLICT with him and each other; something that persists to this day. Yet, God has not abandoned us. He made COVENANTS (promises) to affirm his love for us and presence with us, ultimately sending CHRIST to redeem us and restore our lives to what God originally intended. Those who follow Jesus now live as part of the CHURCH, his Body and Bride, learning and modeling to the world the way of God's Kingdom until the CONSUMMATION of time and the fulfillment of God's plan and design when Jesus will return, the unredeemed shall be judged, and God will create a new heaven and a new earth for his people to inhabit and rule over as he originally intended in creation.

Everything you read in the Bible fits into this gospel story in some way. The sixty-six books of the Bible and hundreds of pages of law, narrative, poetry, teaching, prophecy, and epistles all seek to unpack this story or part thereof. But it is not just the story of the Bible. It is also the story for every human being. For example, some people, apart from Christ, live all of life in chapter two alone. It's a pain-ridden and wounded life, for the most part, filled with conflict and defined by conflict. Others say "Yes" to Christ but "No" to the church and discover that the flourishing life really cannot be lived outside of community. All of us are called and accountable to all of the story as a foundation for faith, hope, and love.

The first three acts are a look back to the fundamental facts of history—God created; conflict and chaos became real; yet God sovereignly, graciously, and purposefully has remained engaged and committed. The last three acts point forward to the hope of restoration and transformation—Christ is still redeeming, the Church is the salt and light of the world, eternity is our glorious hope.

Furthermore, this story reminds us of the ethical imperatives for the flourishing life; the elevation of humanity above all other creation, the pursuit of human purpose (namely, to glorify God), honoring the promises and presence of God, following the teachings and the way of Jesus which he modeled and taught, committing to life in community (the Church) and being motivated and comforted by the prospect of eternal life.

This framework, developed more and more deeply, actually can provide guidance for us on everything from war to bioethics, from politics to civic duty, and from racism to sexism. It touches everything, eventually.

This story feels more powerful than a textbook with chapters on various ethical questions or possibilities. That's the beauty of stories. They have multiple layers, and the best stories are grounded in deep and rich principles that inform broad swaths of life, not just an isolated circumstance. And the gospel is the greatest story, because it is God's story.

Within the CREATION act we can ponder the nature of life. *Origins* — where do we come from? *Purpose* — why are we here? *Design* — how should we relate to each other and the world around us? *Original principles for flourishing* — work, rest, stewardship, dominion, and so much more.

Within the CONFLICT act we start to understand human nature — competition, independence, fear, guilt, shame, sin, and so much more. And the biblical story allows us to be shallow or deep in our ponderings.

Within the COVENANT act we develop convictions about God's persistence, grace, mercy, promises, presence, power, and so much more. His self-disclosure as a God of covenant leads us to learn so much about his character. And what we learn about his character lays out principles for true human flourishing.

Within the CHRIST act we see the hinge of the good news. The first three acts have painted God's plan and our predicament, but this fourth act declares that there is a solution to our problem. Forgiveness is possible. Conflict can be resolved. Transformation can happen. In the Christ act we learn that we are both redeemed AND empowered for new creation living.

This all spills, predictably, into the CHURCH act. And as we read the New Testament, we learn that the Church is a community empowered by the Holy Spirit, through which our lives and our communities can be most fully restored. We learn principles related to worship, selflessness, sacrifice, living for one another, forgiveness, unconditional love, and so much more.

Finally, the CONSUMMATION act lets us dig deep into the nature of eternity, the reality of the unseen world, the power of hope, the certainty of judgment, the significance of vision, and (again) so much more.

It's all here. Every principle that we need for the good life is contained within the layers of the gospel (good news) story. Yes, it can be told in sixty seconds. And then, yes, it can be unpacked and mined for a lifetime. That's what we love about this story, and the chapters to follow will unpack some of the wonders of it.

Chapter Four

CREATION

The story of God in Scripture, which frames the gospel worldview, begins with a loving, transcendent (above and beyond) and immanent (close and nearby) God creating and sustaining all things.

The very first words of Scripture simply declare: "In the beginning God created the heavens and the earth" (Genesis 1:1). Before elaborating on the process, the author lets this simple declaration ground the rest of the story and introduce the main character of the story. We are quick to make this story about us. *Our* salvation. *Our* redemption. *Our* eternal life. While the story of creation shapes our understanding of human origins and purpose, the act of creation is first and foremost about God. Out of the darkness and chaos God spoke light. Where there was formlessness and void, God spoke form and design. The act of creation introduces us to a wise, artistic God and invites us to worship and align our lives with this Creator God.

The declaration of God as maker of heaven and earth, of things seen and unseen, of both the visible and invisible realms, becomes a key identifying factor for God throughout the rest of the story.

Before God's identity as Savior takes shape in Israel's exodus story and before God's identity as lawgiver is established on Mt. Sinai, the act of creation sets the God of Israel apart from all other gods. The act of creation forms God's identity as God Most High.

Shortly after Abraham's calling (Genesis 12), Melchizedek, the king of Salem, blessed him with these words: "Blessed be Abram by God Most High, Creator of heaven and earth" (Genesis 14:19). The God who called Abraham was no ordinary God. This God was the God who created the heavens and the earth. While the exodus narrative and the Mosaic law provide a particularly Jewish identity for God, the identity of Creator places the God of Abraham above all other gods and establishes God as the Father of *all* people and cultures.

In the New Testament, Paul used the identifying feature of Creator to help the Athenians differentiate the God he was proclaiming from the myriad of idols in their city. Using their idol to *An Unknown God*, Paul introduced God this way: "The God who made the world and everything in it is the Lord of heaven and earth and does not live in temples built by human hands" (Acts 17:24). For Paul, the God who created all things, who called Abraham and rescued the Jewish people from slavery in Egypt, is the same God who reaches out to all humanity through the redemptive work of Christ. This creator God is the central character in the story of all humanity. The story starts with him, centers around him at every step of the way, and finishes with him.

Since God is the main character of the story, it is important to first ask ourselves what the act of creation teaches us about God?

The story of creation teaches us that **God is eternal**. Before creation, God exists. The preexistence of God can be seen in the first four words of the story, "In the beginning God..." (Genesis 1:1). Paul stressed that Jesus was "before all things, and in him all things hold together" (Colossians 1:17). God existed before the creation of the heavens and the earth. Furthermore, after creation is finally destroyed and renewed, God will still exist. God is the one constant in this story.

From the story of creation we also learn that **God is self-sufficient**. Existing before the act of creation, God is completely self-sustaining and does not need anything to exist. It is God's self-sufficiency that grounds and sustains all other existence.

In light of God's self-sufficiency the act of creation teaches us that **God is gracious.** Since God does not need creation to exist, as Karl Barth notes, all creation is grace. God did not have to create anything to be God, but in an act of grace God created a world that was separate from himself. God not only created the world but he sustains and orders the world with wisdom and goodness.

Lastly, but by no means exhaustively, because God is the gracious creator and sustainer of all things **God is worthy of our praise**. In the book of the Revelation, the twenty-four elders kneel before the throne and worship God with this song:

You are worthy, our Lord and God, to receive glory and honor and power, for you created all things, and by your will they were created and have their being (Revelation 4:11).

God is worthy to receive glory and honor and power because he is the creator. Note how the act of creation ranks in this celestial song. As the sole creator of all things, God is worthy of praise.

While the act of creation has much more to teach us about God, it also has much to teach us about the nature of the world we love.

The story of creation first teaches us that **the world God created was good** (Genesis 1:10, 12,18,21,25). While we know that this original goodness did not last, it is vitally important for us to recognize the original reality of creation. Without original goodness, creation would not have a better reality to be restored back to.

From the story of creation we also learn that **God created the world with intent and purpose**. God made the earth and everything in it on purpose and with a purpose. Creation is neither accidental nor incidental. The light and the dark each have purpose. The fish of the sea, the birds of the air, and the beasts of the land all have purpose.

The act of creation also helps us understand the fundamental reality of the world in which we live. Because God is the creator and sustainer of all things, **all of creation is dependent on God**. Nothing would be here without God. Nothing would remain without the sustaining providence of God. The Psalmist sings, "The heavens are yours, and yours also the earth; you founded the world and all that is in it" (Psalm 89:11).

While all creation is dependent on God it also **exists to display God's glory and majesty**. John Calvin described all of creation as the theater of God's glory. The angelic beings, impressive in their own right, called to one another in Isaiah's vision: "Holy, holy, holy is the Lord Almighty; the whole earth is full of his glory" (Isaiah 6:3). Calvin stressed "wherever you cast your eyes, there is no spot in the universe wherein you cannot discern at least some sparks of his glory." The Yosemite valley at dusk. The snow-capped peak of Kilaminjaro. The lush river basin of the Amazon. The soft cry of a newborn child. They all show forth the glory of God.

The story of creation also has so much to teach us about what it means to be human. While God declares creation good several times, he declares that **humanity is *very* good** (Genesis 1:31). The creation accounts in both Genesis 1 and 2 show that human beings hold a special place in the created order.

This special status for humanity derives from the unique nature of our creation. Quite distinct from all other creatures, **humanity is created in the image of God** (Genesis 1:26–27). Theologians have debated the exact meaning of being created in the image of God but ultimately it means that all human life is sacred. We have all been created and given equal worth, value, and purpose by God; irrespective of gender, socioeconomic status, or ethnicity.

Furthermore, as God's representatives to this world, we are tasked as **caretakers of God's creation** (Genesis 1:28–30). We are called to have families, to build communities, to wisely care for the fruit of the field and the animals of air, sea, and land.

The act of creation begins the amazing story of God. It reminds us that we are here because of God's power and grace, and helps us give glory to God as our Creator. This amazing story quickly descends into chaos as humanity chooses to rebel against God's good order and pursue its own glory.

Application

1. It matters whether we believe we are created by God on purpose and with a purpose. If we have no intentional *origin*, can we have an intentional *life*?
2. It matters what God is like, and whether we join his story or invite him to join ours. Is life primarily about him or us?
3. It matters that God declares all creation "good" and asks us to steward (not exploit) it. Can we reasonably or responsibly destroy his creation?

Chapter Five

CONFLICT

The story of God begins in a beautiful garden. God inhabits the garden and his goodness permeates every aspect. God has a unique relationship with humanity whom he created in his own image. God walks with them and communes with them as friends. The world and all of humanity are at peace. The man and woman God created, Adam and Eve, live in harmony and without shame (Genesis 2:25).

Sadly, the beauty and perfection of the garden did not last. At a certain point humanity was faced with a decision: to follow God's commands and continue to live in eternal peace or to choose their own way. Humanity chose to follow its own path birthing the violence and strife that are all too common in our world today.

We have chosen to name the second act of the story of God *conflict* because it represents the result of humanity's decision to rebel against God.

Conflict captures the reality of the world east of Eden. We are a people and a world in conflict; in conflict with God and with each other. You do not need to look far to see this conflict. Murder, war, deceit, exploitation, immorality, disorder, and injustices of all kind abound. The news feeds that fill our screens shout the brokenness of humanity.

Far from ignoring the reality of sin and brokenness in our world, the story of God helps us make sense of it. Conflict enters the story in the form of a serpent.

In Genesis 3, Eve encountered a snake who questioned the wisdom and goodness of God ("Did God say...?"; v.1). Doubt crept into her heart and she made a devastating decision. A piece of fruit from a tree in the middle of the garden presented a dual temptation (v.3). On the one hand, there was the temptation to eat it and "be like God" (v.5); a temptation that humanity has faced ever since. On the other hand, Eve saw that the fruit was appealing to the eye and would be good to eat. After taking a bite she offered some to Adam who also ate it (v.6). With this decision the harmony and perfection of God's creation fractured.

The snake and the forbidden fruit represent two core truths of human disobedience: *mistrust of God* and *independence from him*. Skeptical of the wisdom and goodness of God, Adam and Eve pursued their own desires.

While God is still the central character, humans play an important role in this part of the story. Their decision to rebel against God degraded the goodness of creation. Theologically we call this decision *sin*, and sin remains a vital conceptual tool in understanding the current state of our world. In the biblical languages sin refers to missing the mark; specifically, living in ways that do not honor God. When nations rise against other nations, when human beings are enslaved or exploited, when the beauty of creation is destroyed, humanity misses the mark. Cornelius Plantinga defines sin as "culpable shalom breaking." That means that sin is anything that is guilty of destroying the goodness, beauty, well-being, and peace that God intended. In regard to sin, we are all guilty. We stand shoulder to shoulder with all other human beings and confess *mea culpa* (Romans 3:23). God created the world to flourish, to be whole and complete in him, but sin shatters the shalom he intended.

The garden narrative in Genesis 3 describes the tragic moment when this shalom was shattered. In this narrative we see three devastating results of sin that have become the typical experience of human existence: *guilt*, *shame*, and *fear*.

Shortly after Adam and Eve tasted the forbidden fruit, they heard God walking in the garden. As God searched for them, longing to be with them, they hid in fear. God called out for them ("Where are you?"; v.9) and the man responded, "I heard you in the garden, and I was afraid because I was naked; so I hid" (v.10). Unlike the times they spent walking with God before, Adam and Eve were now afraid of God. They were afraid because they felt the weight of the guilt that hung on them. They feared how God might respond to their eating from the tree. Their fear also derived from a new feeling, a companion of guilt but a much different, much deeper sensation, shame. The man doesn't say that they hid from God because they had broken his command but rather because they were naked. Shame moves from the knowledge of *doing wrong* to the existential experience of *being wrong*; from "I have sinned" to "I am unworthy." In the garden that tragic day, Adam and Eve were naked and ashamed.

The narrative in Genesis 3 reveals the shadow side of human existence and helps us understand the brokenness of the world we live in. This brokenness occurs on two fundamental levels.

First, humanity's open and communal relationship with God is severed. Adam and Eve hid in the garden and humanity has been hiding from God ever since. In many ways, we might not even be sure why we are hiding, yet we still hide, like children under a blanket on a stormy night. We did not simply lose this open and communal relationship with God; we rejected him and rebelled against him, choosing our own way over his way.

Second, human relationships are fractured. Jealousy, hatred, lust, and disdain are all too common characteristics of human relationships. We see this displayed in Adam's initial response. When God questioned him concerning the tree in the middle of the garden, Adam directly blamed Eve and indirectly blamed God (v.12). Eve blamed the serpent, and thus began the cycle of judgment and blame that continues to plague humanity today.

The two levels of brokenness (as a result of sin) stand in stark contrast with the two greatest commandments (not the two greatest *suggestions*), drawn from the Old Testament and solidified in the New Testament. Ultimately, we are called by God to love him "with all our heart, soul, mind, and strength" (Deuteronomy 6:5, Matthew 22:37), and to "love your neighbor as yourself" (Leviticus 19:18, Matthew 22:39). All sin finds its root in the reversal of these two fundamental commands.

We experience the conflict and brokenness caused by sin in several ways. Personally, we are riddled with the same guilt, shame, and fear that we saw in the garden. We hide from God in shame and we hide from each other. We often strike first to cover the deep sensation of shame we feel. We also experience conflict in the broken systems of our world. Political, economic, and social structures that marginalize, oppress, and exploit other people showcase the deep brokenness of humanity. This should come as no surprise. The serpent from the garden reemerges in the New Testament as the god of this world, the spirit of disunity and corruption (2 Corinthians 4:4). Sin embeds itself in every dimension of our world. Paul states in the book of Romans that all of creation has been "subject to frustration" and eagerly awaits the final restoration secured by Christ (Romans 8:19–20).

In the Christian community we often try to simplify sin by reducing it to a list of do's and don'ts, but this fails to recognize the true depth of the brokenness caused by sin. It also misses the paradoxical nature of sin.

In Scripture we learn that sin is not just wrong actions it is also expressed through wrong attitudes. Paul notes that even apparently good or neutral actions done with wrong motives still produce the brokenness of sin. This means that sin is much more complex than a simple list. It also means that we are powerless to overcome the devastating effects of sin, both personally and universally. Only God can heal the brokenness of sin and restore shalom to creation.

After Adam and Eve sinned and hid from God, God did something profound and quite surprising. He first declared the curses that their sin would bring on the world, and then he made clothes for them to cover their nakedness (at the expense of a creature's life blood). This was an extraordinary act of grace. The effects of sin and the resulting conflict are painfully evident in our world today, but God does not stand idly by. He continues to cover shame with grace, through the blood of Christ. That's good news.

Conflict is very much the bad news in this story of good news, this gospel, but it is important to understand in order to grasp the full weight and depth of God's grace. God has not stood by and let sin and brokenness win the day. In the next act we see God's redemption plan taking shape. In patience and love, God responded to human sinfulness by entering into a covenant relationship with a people who would play a vital role in bringing salvation to the world.

Application

1. It matters that we identify the origin of our conflict and separation. How does recognition of our innate and fundamental brokenness influence our personal and interpersonal peace?
2. It matters that we frame human conflict as a basic failure to love God and love others. How do these absolute ethics free us rather than restrict us?
3. It matters that we see the pervasive and systemic nature of sin in the world. Why is it important and valuable that we take personal responsibility for our failure and rebellion?

Chapter Six

COVENANT

The story of God's interaction with us could have ended after the second act. In grace and love, God created a good world for us to flourish within, but we rebelled against God, severely altering our relationship with the creator of all that is. Reeling from the choice to rebel against God, we spiraled downward into chaos marked by ever-increasing pride, envy, hatred, and murder.

God could have left us to languish in the consequences of our rebellion, but he had a better plan. Since we were incapable of repairing the broken relationship with God, God himself reached out to us. Though we had rejected him and chosen our own way, God did not abandon us but pursued us with a glorious and purposeful plan.

The third act of the Gospel story is **covenant.**

A covenant is a binding agreement between two parties to faithfully uphold their commitment to each other. In some instances, a covenant can be unilateral; one party makes a promise irrespective of the behavior or commitments of the other party. In the ancient world, it was not unusual for covenants to be established and confirmed by the shedding of blood to underscore the seriousness of the commitment.

Essentially, a covenant is a promise. Time and time again, God has initiated a process of reconciliation with us, evidenced by the various covenants recorded in the Bible.

In the biblical narrative we find six key instances of God making a covenant with humanity: (1) God's covenant with Adam and Eve, (2) God's covenant with Noah, (3) God's covenant with Abraham, (4) God's covenant with Israel (Mosaic Covenant), (5) God's covenant with David, and, finally, (6) God's covenant with humanity through Christ. In each instance we see God taking the first step toward humanity and often reiterating his commitment to restore humanity to the original and perfect goodness of the garden.

In this chapter we will look at these six covenants as we unfold the third act of the gospel worldview.

Adamic Covenant

God's covenant with Adam and Eve began in the garden. After God created Adam and Eve he blessed them and invited them to enjoy and care for the garden (Genesis 1:26–28). He offered them all that the garden provided *except the fruit of the tree in the middle of the garden* (Genesis 2:15–17). We explored how Adam and Eve, as representatives for all of humanity, broke this initial covenant in the second act of the gospel worldview. God responded to the breaking of this covenant with a judgment and a promise.

In Genesis 3:15, God rendered judgment (curses) on Adam, Eve, the serpent, and all creation, but he also promised a future savior who would thoroughly defeat the serpent; a promise that will be fulfilled through Christ in the final covenant.

Noahic Covenant

God's covenant with Noah and his family came after a great flood, which God used to judge the increasing wickedness of humanity. God rescued

Noah and his family from this judgment because Noah "found favor in the eyes of the Lord" (6:8). Furthermore, after the flood waters receded he made them a promise to never judge the earth in this manner again (Genesis 8:20 – 9:17).

God's covenant with Noah and his family marks a covenant with all humanity, echoing back to God's intention for Adam and Eve in the garden. God charged Noah and his family to multiply and fill the earth. They were also called to care for the earth and the animals that were rescued with them. However, God's covenant with Noah and the rest of humanity was one-sided (unilateral). God knew that humanity would continue to fall short and rebel against his design for the world, yet God did not put any conditions on the covenant. His promise extended to all future generations from Noah and was accompanied with a sign of the covenant, a rainbow, to remind humanity of his continual faithfulness.

Abrahamic Covenant

The next major covenant we see in Scripture is the covenant God made with Abraham. In that covenant God singled out a particular family among all humanity to enter into an everlasting partnership which would eventually bring salvation to the whole world. The Abrahramic covenant began with the call of Abram (Genesis

12). God promised to bless Abram, to make his name great, and to make him into a great nation (vv.2–3).

Unlike the Noahic covenant, Abram had a part to fulfill. God asked him to leave his country, his people, and his father's household and go to a land that would be revealed later by God. In an act of great faith, Abram left his own people and family and followed God to an unknown land.

Years passed and Abram, still childless and landless, questioned how God would fulfill his promise to him. God reasserted his covenant with Abram and gave him a sign. God asked Abram to bring to him a heifer, a goat, and a ram, as well as a dove and a young pigeon (Genesis 15:9). Abram cut the heifer, the goat, and the ram in half in what scholars note as a traditional cutting covenant ceremony where two parties walk through the middle of the halved animals to seal the covenant between them. After laying out the animals, Abram fell into a deep sleep and a very interesting thing occurred. Abram and God did not both walk through the halved animals, rather a smoking firepot and a blazing torch passed through the animals (v.17). In this unique story, God showed that he is the one who makes and maintains the covenant with Abram. God, then, mapped out the land that would be given to Abram.

More years passed. Abram had grown in wealth and reputation but he and his wife Sarai remained childless. They had even taken matters into their own hands and forced a child at the expense of their servant Hagar, yet God reassured them that his original promise would be fulfilled. God appeared to Abram again and reasserted his promise to make Abram the father of many nations. To underscore the coming fulfillment of the promise, God changed Abram's name to Abraham and his wife Sarai's name to Sarah, and marked the covenant with a new sign: the sign of circumcision. Within a year, when Abraham was one hundred years old and Sarah was around ninety, Isaac, the child of promise, was born and along with him the beginnings of the nation of Israel.

Mosaic Covenant

From the time of Isaac forward, Abraham's descendants grew into a large family and amassed sizable wealth. It is difficult though to consider this a time of blessing. The family was plagued by infighting, brother turning on brother, eventually leading to enslavement in Egypt. While they were in Egypt, laboring under harsh conditions, they cried out to God and "God heard their groaning and he remembered his covenant with Abraham, with Isaac and with Jacob" (Exodus 2:24).

God remembered his covenant with Abraham's descendants and chose Moses to lead the people out of slavery, a man from among them that had his own complicated story. When God liberated his people from slavery in Egypt, he established a more formal covenant with them captured in the Torah or Law. Above all, God promised again that he alone would be their God and that they would be his people (Exodus 6:7).

God promised to lead the Israelites to the land he promised to Abraham, Isaac, and Jacob. Through Moses, God laid out rules for the people to follow as a way to remind them daily of the covenant he had made with them.

The journey out of slavery was not a straight path from Egypt to the promised land. The Jewish people were hard of heart and often rebelled against God. In fact, most of those who were rescued from Egypt did not make it to the promised land, including Moses, because they had not trusted God. They died in the wilderness during forty years of wandering. It was their children who entered the promised land. Nevertheless, through it all, God remained faithful, eventually establishing the people in the land.

Davidic Covenant

King David represented the pinnacle of the nation of Israel in the land God promised to Abraham. The people were prosperous and filled the land.

King David was a strong and courageous leader, but he was far from perfect. He won many battles and was zealous for God. He desperately wanted to build a temple for God, but David was not the leader that God was going to use. He too struggled with faithfully fulfilling the requirements of the covenant given through Moses. Despite David's failures, God promised him that he would raise up one of his offspring, someone from David's own body, to rule over God's people, and that through him David's throne would be established forever (2 Samuel 7:12–16).

God did use one of David's sons, King Solomon, to build the temple in Jerusalem, and though he was wise and widely celebrated by the people, not even he was the one promised in the covenant. After Solomon, king after king only succeeded in moving the people further away from God, resulting in both the destruction of the temple and captivity of the people.

Long after the time of David, the people were still waiting for the one promised, and still waiting for the everlasting kingdom.

New Covenant

All of the prior covenants God made with humanity and the people of Israel specifically lead to this final covenant, a covenant secured through the life, death, and resurrection of his son, Jesus.

With this New Covenant, Jesus ushered in a new way for humanity to relate to God. The New Covenant breaks ethnic and cultural barriers to provide a way for all humanity to be restored to the right relationship with God. In many ways, the New Covenant ushers in the blessing of the whole world first promised in the Abrahamic covenant. Like all of the prior covenants, the New Covenant is first initiated by the action of God. John 3:16 famously notes, "For God so loved the world that he gave his one and only Son, that whoever believes in him shall not perish but have eternal life."

Jesus came to earth, in the line of David, to announce the coming of the kingdom of God and to show God's immense love for humanity. In his life and ministry, Jesus taught the people, often in parables, what the kingdom of heaven is like.

He also displayed the power of the kingdom in a variety of miraculous signs.

The death of Jesus on a Roman cross sealed the covenant with his blood (Matthew 26:28) and the resurrection signified God's triumph over death (1 Corinthians 15:55–57).

The New Covenant is the good news of the gospel worldview. God has not abandoned us. When we trust him alone and entirely, we receive grace. Our sins are forgiven. Death no longer has the final word. The Kingdom of heaven is at hand.

In the gospel worldview, Act 3, the act of covenant, reflects decisive moments in the storyline when God responded to our rebellion with love, mercy, and action. Far from rejecting us, God repeatedly made covenants to bring salvation and the kingdom of heaven. This covenantal action of the Old Testament culminates with the incarnation of Jesus and the New Covenant. In him alone we find our true source of hope. In him, we find new and everlasting life.

Application

1. It matters that God makes covenants. What other evidence would we have for his

personal engagement with us and commitment to us?

2. It matters which covenants (promises) God chooses to make to us. Why do promises of safety, sovereignty, community, salvation, and transformation make a difference?

3. It matters that God's covenants are basically promises, not threats. In what way might this encourage and inspire our own lives and choices?

Chapter Seven

CHRIST

In Act 4, the gospel worldview centers around the incarnation of Jesus Christ. Incarnation simply means "to make or become flesh." With the incarnation, the God who created the world steps into creation by taking on flesh, by becoming human. With the incarnation, God steps into the conflicted-ridden world that is racked by sin and separation. With the incarnation, the covenants God created with humanity are finally fulfilled. In Christ, the God who created the heavens and the earth is revealed in a decisive way.

The Gospel of John begins with this simple, yet powerful message: "In the beginning was the Word, and the Word was with God, and the

Word was God" (John 1:1). John proclaims that Jesus is the Word of God. Jesus is God revealed to us. Jesus is God's message to us; a message of love and acceptance. Jesus, as the Word of God, proclaims to the world that the conflict is over. God's love has prevailed. God has remained faithful to the covenants and provided a way for salvation and reconciliation.

Jesus is not merely a messenger sent from God. Jesus *is* God. John goes on to note that through Jesus "all things were made; without him nothing was made that has been made" (John 1:3). Jesus is not separate from the God of Act 1, the act of creation. This means that the God we worship and serve, the God revealed in the gospel worldview, is much more complex than a solitary being demanding our fealty.

Central to the gospel worldview is the affirmation that the Father, the Son (Jesus), along with the Holy Spirit are God. Theologically, we use the term trinity.

Trinity is a way of understanding the one essence of God in the three persons. This theological affirmation has powerful implications. God knows how to be in relationship with others, how to be loyal to others, how to love others, because by nature God is a communion of three persons. God is love (1 John 4:8) and because of that love he came into our world in Christ. Eugene Peterson paraphrases the Gospel of John this way, "The Word became flesh and blood, and moved into the neighborhood" (John 1:14; MSG).

In Scripture, we see these two aspects of Jesus' nature described; his deity and humanity. Let's first look at the affirmations for the deity of Christ.

Paul stresses that in Christ "all the fullness of the deity lives in bodily form" (Colossians 2:9). While it is true that Jesus does not often refer to himself as God, in the Gospel of John he makes a strong inference: "Very truly I tell you,' Jesus answered, 'before Abraham was born, I am!'" (John 8:58).

Perhaps the strongest evidence for the divinity of Christ occurs when Jesus himself performs actions that are only attributed to God. In the Gospel of Mark, while healing a paralytic man, Jesus also forgives the man's sins, a prerogative reserved for God (Mark 2:1–12). The religious leaders present understood the claim Jesus was making and scoffed, "'Why does this fellow talk like that? He's blaspheming! Who can forgive sins but God alone?'" (Mark 2:7)

Along with these claims of divinity, we also see a very human Jesus. Jesus' birth by the virgin Mary, while miraculous, also shows that Jesus was born of a woman (Matthew 1:18–25). Jesus did not mysteriously appear in the story as a fully-grown man. He was born. He became a child and the Gospel of Luke notes that "the child grew and became strong; he was filled with wisdom, and the grace of God was on him" (Luke 2:40). If the incarnation was only about the cross, an aspect of Jesus' story we'll discuss in this chapter, he could have simply appeared at the age of thirty, and proceeded immediately with his ministry, death, and resurrection. But Jesus came to earth as a baby, a very human baby. He had to be fed, changed, and clothed. And he had to grow and learn. He experienced fully what it means to be human, yet perfectly righteous and without sin. He experienced thirst (John 19:28), hunger (Matthew 4:2), and being tired (John 4:6). In many ways, he was a typical college student attending an early morning class.

Jesus also endured other human experiences: being misunderstood by his family (Mark 3:21), betrayal at the hand of a friend (Mark 14:45), and ultimately death (Matthew 27:45–56). The book of Hebrews stresses, "For this reason he had to be made like [us], fully human in every way" (Hebrews 2:17). Scripture is clear. Jesus was not impersonating a human but rather he took on the form of humanity to his very depths and truly lived out the human experience in every way.

The book of Hebrews goes on in this very same verse to underscore that Jesus became a human being "in order that he might become a merciful and faithful high priest in service to God, and that he might make atonement for the sins of the people" (v.17). While it is tempting to jump straight to the atonement aspect of the reasoning, the first part is just as important. Jesus became human in order to become both merciful and faithful. By experiencing what it means to be human, with all of its complexities, Jesus better embodies mercy. He knows what we go through. He understands the daily struggles we face, and he responds with mercy and grace. By becoming human, Jesus was also able to model faithfulness for us. He faithfully fulfilled the call of God the Father, even when that call led to an excruciating death on the cross. With mercy and faithfulness, Christ went to the cross to make atonement for the sins of the people.

By using the word atonement, the author of Hebrews is referring to the Jewish celebration of the Day of Atonement (Leviticus 23:27–28), the pinnacle of all of the Jewish festivals.

On the Day of Atonement, the high priest would make a sacrifice in order to atone for, or cover, the sins of the Jewish people. Christ's death on the cross stands as the final sacrifice which covers the sin of everyone who confesses him as Lord. But atonement is more than just having our sins forgiven. Christ's death and resurrection mark his victory in the war against sin and death (Colossians 2:15). Christ conquers the powers of this world through his death and resurrection. The conflict depicted in Act 2 of the gospel worldview is resolved. Through the cross and resurrection Christ secures for us the everlasting forgiveness of God (Romans 3:25–26). On the cross, Christ loudly proclaims the grace and love of God for all humanity and again models faithfulness for us (John 3:16).

The faithful model Christ provides for us with his life and death is beautifully captured by Paul in his letter to the Philippians:

> Christ, being in very nature God, did not consider equality with God something to be used to his own advantage; rather, he made himself nothing by taking the very nature of a servant, being made in human likeness. And being found in appearance as a man, he humbled himself by becoming obedient to death – even death on a cross! (Philippians 2:6–8).

Here Paul provides the simple yet profound key to the incarnation: humility. Jesus, being one with the Father, humbled himself to become human, to serve, to be scorned, and to eventually die.

While Christ's death on the cross won the victory over sin and death, it also stands as a model for how we should live our lives.

Many times, we are satisfied with accepting the atonement for our sins without truly modeling our lives after Christ. The goal of this great story of God is not simply our ultimate salvation and the gift of eternal life. The goal is that we would be made right with God (what the Bible calls *justification*) and our lives would change here on earth (what the Bible calls *sanctification*); that our inner selves would be shaped into Christ's likeness more and more, long before the end of our lives, and long before the end of this story.

Act 4 is the pivotal act in this gospel story. God has come to earth and personally understands the human experience.

Act 4 proclaims the good news that God has not abandoned humanity. A savior has come. But the story doesn't end here. Surprisingly, Jesus didn't remain on earth. He ascended to the Father and gave us the gift of the Holy Spirit to dwell in us and empower us to carry on the work of the kingdom of heaven.

The next act, Act 5, the Church, picks up the story after Jesus returns to the Father and reveals the part that we get to play in the story. We are invited to be Christ's body in the world.

Application

1. It matters that we acknowledge Christ as Lord of all; all creation and all of us. How does a life submitted to his Lordship differ from one that rebels against it?
2. It matters that Jesus is fully God and fully human; that he models perfect humanity. Why is such a model so important?
3. It matters that Christ has made atonement for our sins; that he has broken both the power and the penalty of sin. How does this shape our experience of guilt and shame?

Chapter Eight

CHURCH

The fifth Act of the gospel worldview tells the story of the formation of the church as Christ's body in the world. This act begins with a final meeting between Jesus and his disciples. In this final meeting, Jesus commissioned his followers to take this message of good news wherever they might go, to the ends of the earth. Shortly after giving this commission, Jesus bodily ascended to the Father in front of his disciples.

At first read, the ascension might strike us as odd. Did Jesus really need to float away from his disciples, as if God were spatially located in the clouds? When you think more deeply about it though, it is clear that Jesus needed to show his disciples in a very real way that he was going back to the Father and would not be with them in physical form anymore.

After the resurrection, Jesus appeared to his followers over a period of forty days. He shared final stories with them. He ate with them. He allowed them to touch his scarred body. He also walked through locked doors (John 20:19) and vanished only to reappear somewhere else (Luke 24:31).

Jesus did not have to physically float to heaven but he did need to show his disciples that he would not be there anymore to teach, or to heal, *as they had experienced him thus far.* While he would be with them always (Matthew 28:20) by means of the Holy Spirit, he was passing the ball to them. It was now up to them (empowered and led by the Holy Spirit) to carry this gospel to the rest of the world.

In his final commissioning, Jesus promised the presence and power of the Holy Spirit. "But you will receive power when the Holy Spirit fills you; and you will be my witnesses in Jerusalem, and in all Judea and Samaria, and to the ends of the earth" (Acts 1:8).

The Holy Spirit would empower, guide, and sustain Jesus' followers. Jesus also did not want his followers to be lone messengers of God's love and grace, but rather to be in communities he called the church.

In Scripture, the word church comes from the Greek term *ekklesia*. For many people, especially in the English-speaking world, the word church conjures up images of buildings or places of worship, but the original meaning of the Greek term is much more powerful. Any time the word *ekklesia* is used in the New Testament it always references a gathered group of people, not a building or location. The church was and always will be the assembled people of God, not a building or organization.

In today's world, it is easy to get confused about what the church should look like and what the church should be doing. While the beauty of the church is that it can take many different forms, the earliest descriptions of the church provide helpful characteristics of the core nature and purpose of the church.

The church first began to form after the experience of the Holy Spirit at the Day of Pentecost. In Acts 2, we read that the earliest fellowship of Christian believers devoted themselves to the apostle's teaching (teaching primarily about Jesus and the good news of the kingdom), the breaking of bread, to fellowship, and to prayer (Acts 2:42). These earliest Christians shared their possessions with each other and took care of each other's needs (vv.44–45). They worshiped together daily and met in each other's homes (v.46).

The beauty of this description of the early church lies in its simplicity. This early community of believers was not trying to build a large organization, or increase their social standing. They were simply responding to the life-changing message of Jesus and coming together to worship, learn more about the message of Jesus, and care for each other. While the church can take many forms, these characteristics represent the core mission.

As we have seen, Jesus himself established the church and gave it a primary mission. While talking with his disciples one day he asked them who the people thought he was. They replied that some thought he was John the Baptist. Others thought he was Elijah. He then asked them a pointed question, "Who do you say I am?" (Matthew 16:15). Peter answered quickly, "You are the Messiah, the son of the living God" (v.16). Jesus' response to Peter gives us an interesting insight concerning the church. "Blessed are you, Simon son of Jonah, for this was not revealed to you by flesh and blood, but by my Father in heaven. And I tell you that you are Peter, and on this rock I will build my church, and the gates of Hades will not overcome it" (vv.17–18). Jesus not only changes Peter's name, he puts him at the center of the establishment of the church. Earlier he had promised that Peter would have "the keys of the kingdom of heaven" (Matthew 16:19) and we see Peter preach the inaugural sermon to Jews (Acts 2:14-36) and later Gentiles (Acts 10:34-43).

We learn two extremely important facts about the church here. One, the church is Jesus' church — "I will build my church." The church does not belong to the pastor, priest, or any governing authority. The church is the body of Christ in the world and flows from him. Second, the church is not a stationary institution but rather a movement of Christ-followers. Note that Jesus said the gates of Hades will not stop it. Jesus is saying that not even the door to the realm of the dead will stop the church. He is also saying that the church should not be afraid to go to the darkest places because they have been established by him and carry his protection.

One of the main metaphors used for the church in the New Testament is the metaphor of the body (Romans 12, 1 Corinthians 12, Ephesians 4, Hebrews 13). The metaphor of a body is an apt way to describe the nature of the church. A body is made up of many different parts. Each part has its own function and one part is not more important than the others. The church, as an assembled group of Christ-followers, is made up of many different members but is at the same time a united body of believers.

In his paraphrase of 1 Corinthians, Eugene Peterson draws out the powerful point that highly visible parts of the body are only significant because they are a part of the whole body. One part on its own is not only bad but would be monstrous. "For no matter how significant you are, it is only because of what you are a part of. An enormous eye or a gigantic hand wouldn't be a body, but a monster. What we have is one body with many parts, each its proper size and in its proper place. No part is important on its own" (1 Corinthians 12:19–20, The Message).

The New Testament also stresses that each member of the body has its own set of gifts. Various different gifts are listed in Scripture (Romans 12; 1 Corinthians 12). Some people have the gift of wisdom. Some have the gift of knowledge. Some the gift of faith. Others have the gift of teaching, and so on. It is important to remember that these lists are not exhaustive. Rather, Paul is stressing that each of us have something to offer to the whole body of Christ.

Another metaphor used for the church in the New Testament is the metaphor of a bride. This metaphor has many facets. As the bride of Christ, the church is set apart for him alone. This means that the church is called to be loyal only to him. The church's loyalty is not demanded by an absent bridegroom though. Christ gave himself up for the church in the highest act of self-sacrifice and unconditional love (Ephesians 5:25). Sadly, the church has not always been a faithful bride, but Jesus' love is never-ending and always forgiving. That means that you do not have to be perfect to be a part of the church, because the church isn't perfect. Through repentance and contrition, the church remains faithful.

The fifth act of the gospel worldview is an important part of the greater story of God because it is the act where believers today enter the story. As believers, we are members of the body of Christ. We are set apart as the bride of Christ. We are the church and God has gifted each one of us to play a vital role in the life of the church whether our gifts are highly visible or more behind the scenes. The question posed by this act is not if we fit into this story, but rather it asks us to consider *where* we fit in God's good story.

Application

1. It matters that we understand the basic qualities and characteristics of the church (the Body of Christ). How does this community of believers help guide our thinking and form our souls?
2. It matters that the church belongs to Christ and not to us. How might this shape our expectations, systems, structures, and efforts in this community?
3. It matters that the Holy Spirit sustains, equips, inspires, and empowers the church. Why does this truth make such a difference if we embrace it?

Chapter Nine

CONSUMMATION

The sixth and final act of the gospel worldview is *consummation*. This act is the culmination of God's wonderful story of the redemption of humanity through Jesus Christ. In this final act, we look forward to a time when God will complete this work of redemption and restore the earth back to its original beauty and goodness. Through the previous five acts of the gospel story we have discovered God's ultimate plan to restore humanity and all of creation to the full glory he originally intended. Humanity will one day reflect the image, character, and glory of God in Christ without distortion. While we do not yet live in that space, all of time and history is pointing towards the Day of the Lord when those who belong to the family of God will receive eternal life and inherit the new heavens and new earth. The old will pass away, and the new things will come. Christ, the lamb that was slain, will reign upon the throne with justice and grace, and his people, resurrected to never die again, will once again steward God's creation.

In Paul's first letter to the church in Corinth, he ends his beautiful description of love with this statement: "And now these three remain: faith, hope and love. But the greatest of these is love" (1 Corinthians 13:13). The sixth and final act of the gospel worldview particularly builds upon this powerful triad. We trust that Jesus will return and restore creation to its original beauty takes faith. Even when circumstances appear bleak, Jesus' return and promised restoration offers us hope. Most importantly, the return of Christ proclaims God's love for his creation. But of these three qualities, hope serves a unique role in this final act.

Fear is often the first response to the thought of Christ's return and the end of the world as we know it. Prophetic visions in books like Daniel or Revelation can be quite frightening to read, but we must remember that the primary purpose of the prophetic visions of the end times was to inspire hope in the reader. God is not going to let the pain and suffering of this world last forever. God has promised to return and heal the earth. And ultimately God is victorious, though it may appear grim now. Hope is more than mere wishful thinking about the future though. Henri Nouwen defines biblical hope as "trust that God will fulfill God's promises to us in a way that leads us to true freedom." We have hope because our hope is grounded on the promises of God and we have faith that God is able to do what he has promised.

Our hope has multiple dimensions. First, God's triumph over sin and death has personal implications. As individuals we are saved by God's victory. Hope also has a corporate dimension. We are not just individuals seeking salvation. As we saw in the fifth act of the gospel worldview, we have been called into a family. As God's family, we hope in our collective salvation and restoration. And finally, Christian hope has a cosmic dimension. God has promised not only to rescue us but to restore and renew his total creation.

In both Isaiah and Revelation we see the future promise of "new heavens and a new earth" (Isaiah 65:17; Revelation 21:1). Paul stresses in his letter to the Romans that all of creation is groaning, waiting for this restoration (Romans 8:22). While it can feel like this future restoration might never happen, Paul evokes hope again and teaches us a valuable lesson. "For in this hope we were saved. But hope that is seen is no hope at all. Who hopes for what they already have?" (Romans 8:24) We do not hope in something that we have already fully experienced. Hope bridges the gap between the agony of our present world and the promised kingdom.

The Bible provides several symbols of hope that help us better understand the nature of hope and its role in the gospel worldview.

One Christian symbol of hope centers on the return of Christ. Just as Christ came to earth, he has promised to return and has called us to expectantly wait for his return (John 14:1-3). This teaches us that Christian hope is hope in a person, specifically the person of Jesus. We do not have blind hope just as we do not have blind faith. We can have hope for the future because our hope is found in Christ. Each time we remember what he has already done in history, we strengthen our hope for what he will do in the future. This symbol asks us to trust in his promise to complete the work of salvation.

Another symbol of hope centers on resurrection. Christ's saving work is based on both his sacrifice on the cross and his victory over sin and death in the resurrection. Paul stressed the significance of

Christ's resurrection to the church at Corinth. "And if Christ has not been raised, your faith is futile; you are still in your sins" (1 Corinthians 15:17).

Through his own resurrection, Christ offers us hope that sin and death have been defeated. Death is not final. We can have everlasting life because of Christ. It is important to remember that this resurrection is about the whole person; soul, spirit, and body. The resurrection also embraces those already dead and those yet unborn. Paul encouraged the believers in Thessalonica that those who die before Christ's return are not excluded from the kingdom (1 Thessalonians 4:13–18). Or, as theologian Karl Barth stressed, "The goal of human life is not death, but resurrection."

Another symbol of hope found in the gospel story is the symbol of a final judgment. The symbol of a final judgment may seem void of hope and to many it conjures feelings of fear and dread. We must remember though that this is not a symbol of vindictive punishment, but of justice. Just as God has promised, he will make right what has been so terribly wrong on earth. He will end the pain and suffering and hold perpetrators both responsible and accountable.

While it is easy to cheer on God holding others accountable, we must remember that we all will be held accountable in this final judgment. This may not sound very hopeful and if we were left on our own it would be a terrible event. However, the good news of the Gospel is that our judge is also our savior. The God who judges is also the God who in mercy and love provided the way of salvation. God does not judge us as one removed from the human experience, but one who deeply felt our pain through the incarnation. In this light, we can approach this final judgment with hope, knowing that God has come to our defense and covers us with his righteousness.

Consummation, the sixth and final act of the gospel worldview, culminates the good news of God's story with the hope of the final fulfillment of God's promises. From the garden in the beginning of the story, the scene of both the creation and the fall of humanity, God has consistently promised humanity and all of creation that he will restore all things and make things right. As we see in the story, he begins this process by reaching out to Abraham with a covenant to form a people that would carry his name and message of hope into the world. This message peaks with the incarnation of Christ. Through the work of Christ on the cross and in the resurrection, sin and death are defeated. The conflict was ultimately won but the battle continues. As Christ ascended back to the Father he promised to return and he has empowered his people, the church, to act as agents of reconciliation in the world. This is where we find ourselves in the story at the present moment. But one day Christ will return and God's remarkable story of salvation and restoration will be complete. Until then, we are called to share the hope inspired by this story.

Application

1. It matters that we have a perspective of eternity. How else can we find hope in suffering, grief, or loss?
2. It matters that we believe in the resurrection. Why would faith be vain without it?
3. It matters that we believe in the restoration of all things, by God. How might this plan and hope impact some of our daily choices?

Chapter Ten

Final Reflections

We live in a time when a cohesive worldview is difficult to identify or articulate. All kinds of philosophies swirl around us.

Some people embrace a secular humanism that eliminates any divine element and puts human life at the front and center of everything. This worldview looks only to human beings for meaning and hope, and generally ends in disappointment. If you are exposed to the best of humanity, you might become mildly optimistic. But if you take just a moment to watch the news and hear the stories from around the world, there is little to inspire us and far more to frighten us.

Some people embrace a worldview marked by hedonism and selfishness. "Eat, drink, and be merry, for tomorrow we die" is their catchcry. "Party hard! Play hard! Have a good time and look after yourself!" Based on the doom and gloom that cable news pumps out relentlessly, we can understand this choice to disengage and simply chase pleasure while it can be found. In this worldview, life has no real meaning or direction, and there is no framework for understanding or enduring suffering. Nor does this philosophy help us live more nobly and successfully in marriages or friendships. It fails at every significant level.

Yet other people find meaning and passion in activism and advocacy. They are ready to fight for rights (their own and others) and devote themselves to almost any struggle for equality and justice. But without a framework for understanding human nature, and without clarity about an end goal, their struggle can become marked by aggression and hostility, the very qualities against which they protest. Equality and justice matter, but there must be an ethical framework larger than these two qualities alone, or the ends will justify the means and ironically (as we have seen many times) the result is not the elimination of inequality or injustice but the mere reversal or transference of it to another group.

We could continue to examine a range of philosophies, ideologies, and worldviews in Western culture. But the gospel worldview speaks deeply and profoundly to us all.

We must insist that a meaningful worldview provide coherent answers to the following questions: Where did I come from? Why am I here? How should I live? And where am I going?

Alongside these fundamental questions, is one more question of profound significance. It is the question of hope. Our common human experience makes it obvious that human nature is intrinsically selfish, greedy, lustful, jealous, prone to anger and violence, prejudiced, and proud. None of these elements build our lives. To the contrary, they isolate us and divide us. If there is hope for humanity, surely it is not simply in political constructs, economic models, or civic systems. If we might reasonably imagine a changed world, we must first imagine changed individuals. Surely then, we will desire a worldview that addresses ways and means by which we might be individually transformed (without eliminating our individuality) and thus collectively helped.

If you have been tracking with us through this book, then you know by now that we believe deeply and resolutely that the gospel worldview provides the only consistent and comprehensive good news.

CREATION: We have been created on purpose and for a purpose, by God who gives us purpose and transcends our limitations.

CONFLICT: The brokenness, sin, separation, and suffering in our lives is not the plan or intent of God, but the choice of our human forebears, and ourselves day-by-day.

COVENANT: God remains engaged in our world, constantly reaching out to all of humanity, equally and without favoritism, seeking to restore and redeem us.

CHRIST: Jesus, the Son of God, came to redeem us and deliver us from the curse and penalty of sin. He shows us perfect humanity and teaches us how to live.

CHURCH: The church (at its best) models a community of people who are uniquely called, individually valuable, hope-filled, joy-filled, selflessly sacrificial, loving and, above all, empowered and transformed by the Spirit of God within them. The work of Christ to redeem us, and the ministry of the Spirit to transform us, is the hope of the world.

CONSUMMATION: Eternity is not formless or void. Nor is it disembodied or impersonal. The suffering of this present age is not worthy to be compared with the glory that will be revealed to, through, and in the children of God.

As you might notice, everything about this gospel worldview addresses and offers a solution to the partial concerns of the competing ideologies of our day.

Hinduism is fatalistic and nihilistic. You have no way to improve yourself or to improve your station in this life. You get what you deserve. There is no grace, and little meaningful hope. There is certainly nothing to change a culture or change the world. The gospel worldview speaks powerfully to every deficiency of Hinduism.

Taoism advocates humility and a form of religious piety, calling its adherents to live in balance with the Tao, or the universe. It believes in spiritual immortality, but the spirit of the body simply joins the universe after death. Once again, individuality is significantly suppressed, human effort becomes the key to tranquility, and eternity is depersonalized. There is no real meaning, value, or purpose to individual lives. By contrast, the gospel worldview offers explanation for our basic human experience and declares a way forward that both restores, values, and empowers us for transformation. We look beyond ourselves, not merely within ourselves, for hope.

Buddhism recognizes suffering as core to the human experience. Such suffering is deemed to be the result of desire and attachment. Consequently, Buddhism advocates basic ethical convictions such as "Don't kill (anything)" and "Don't take (steal)" but teaches that we can only minimize our suffering by lessening our attachments. Eventually, through meditation, spiritual and physical labor, and good behavior we will achieve a level of disembodied enlightenment (nirvana) where there is neither suffering, desire, nor a sense of self. By contrast (again), the gospel worldview honors our humanity and makes God the center of our story. There's nothing disembodied, impersonal, detached, or disengaged about it.

We could continue, but perhaps you see the point here. It's not just the political and social ideologies of our day that fail the test of true hope and helpfulness; the major religious systems and philosophies also fall substantially short.

This is His Story

Perhaps this gospel worldview of which we have written needs one final qualification.

We might easily conclude that the gospel worldview is merely another human fabrication, another ethical system with religious overtones, another meritorious model to consider; just another competitor for our consideration.

Nothing could be further from our intent.

The gospel worldview is not of our making. It is not a watertight philosophy or an attractive ideology. It is, first and foremost, derived from

God's Word, not human wisdom. Who could have, or would have, derived such a perspective of humanity and human history? Who in their best moments would have argued for a crucified God (the ultimate expression of shame and weakness) as the hinge of history? This is not our story but God's story. We are not, surprisingly enough, the central character of human history. He is. But, true to his character and nature, he is utterly faithful to all which he has created. He made us, redeemed us, sustains us, transforms us, and prepares a place for us, but he does so without sacrificing his sovereignty or diminishing our dignity.

Finally, this gospel story and gospel worldview finds its bedrock in both truth and faith.

All that we have written is true. You, dear reader, are created on purpose and with purpose. You are unique and valued by God. Your life matters. You have a calling and you can have hope. Christ can change you and change everything about you and for you. You have a future. And all of this means that we will live differently. These are truths.

But the real appropriation of the gospel goes well beyond a mental assent. You might agree with the narrative we have retold in this book. You might like the idea of living with such freedom, affirmation, love, joy, and hope. But it comes not by saying yes to the story but by saying yes to the author of the story.

The Bible tells us that Christ Jesus was in the beginning. He created all things and all things were created for him. He sustains us, and apart from him nothing exists. And whether we understand all of the nuances of this story or not, the key to redemption and transformation in our lives, marriages, families, and communities is to trust Christ; trust him with our wounds and pain; trust him with our hopes and aspirations; trust him with our dreams and disappointments; trust him with our consolation and our desolation. It is this life of trust that allows us to enter deeply, personally, and gloriously into his story; a story that began before the creation of this world and extends beyond the end of this world.

Our hope is that you'll join us and lean into this life of faith; this life of deepening trust. Therein lies our great and true hope. Will you turn away from everything that destroys and divides us, change your mind about the claims of Christ, and say yes to him? Will you embrace the thoughtful gospel and the Author of the Story?

Made in the USA
Monee, IL
04 July 2023

38506065R00059